EL TOVAR

AT GRAND CANYON NATIONAL PARK

by Christine Barnes

Photography by Fred Pflughoft & David Morris

W.W.WEST

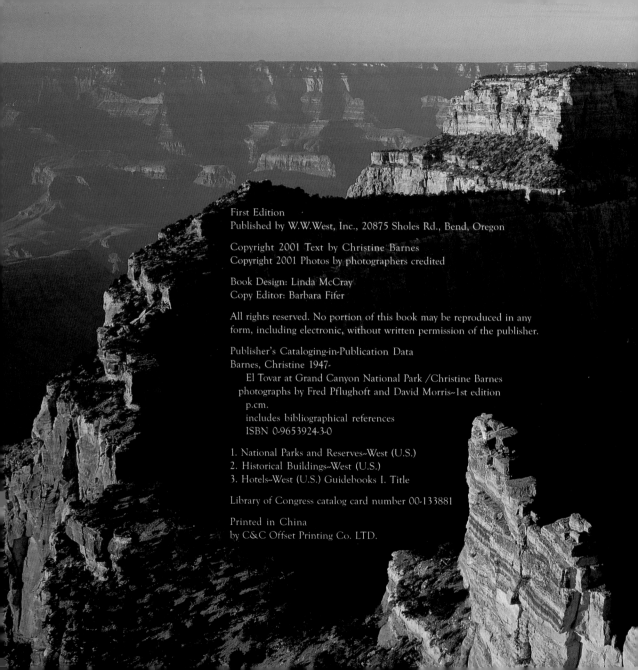

First Edition
Published by W.W.West, Inc., 20875 Sholes Rd., Bend, Oregon

Copyright 2001 Text by Christine Barnes
Copyright 2001 Photos by photographers credited

Book Design: Linda McCray
Copy Editor: Barbara Fifer

Publisher's Cataloging-in-Publication Data
Barnes, Christine 1947-
    El Tovar at Grand Canyon National Park /Christine Barnes
  photographs by Fred Pflughoft and David Morris~1st edition
    p.cm.
    includes bibliographical references
    ISBN 0-9653924-3-0

1. National Parks and Reserves~West (U.S.)
2. Historical Buildings~West (U.S.)
3. Hotels~West (U.S.) Guidebooks I. Title

Library of Congress catalog card number 00-133881

Printed in China
by C&C Offset Printing Co. LTD.

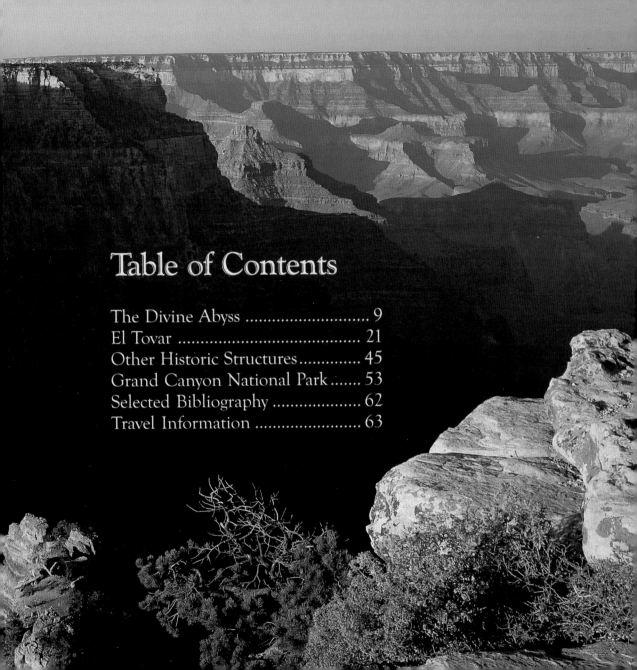

Table of Contents

The Divine Abyss

By the late 1800s, Americans were giddy in their enthusiasm for the West. Explorers had mapped out the terrain, and their journals and articles described land like no other. Adventurous travelers survived horseback, wagon or stagecoach rides with stiff upper lips and leathered backsides, but it was rail travel that opened stretches of the unknown to people hungry for the experience. But laying rails, attaining rights of way, and wagering on the volatile transportation game was a political, logistical and costly affair.

Like other railways, the Atchison, Topeka & Santa Fe was opening up exotic American landscapes. The long reaches of color-swathed desert of the Southwest were among the last to be explored, and the tour de force of that landscape, the Grand Canyon, was a destination to be reckoned with.

Formed by the erosive powers of the Colorado River over a period of 10,000,000 years, its layer upon layer of geologic history was a formidable specimen for interpretation—and awe. Native peoples first explored the region perhaps 10,000 years ago. Zuni, Hopi, Navajo, Havasupai, Hualapai and Mojave tribes were among those who lived, farmed, hunted and built their homes and pueblos in the semi-arid Southwest.

ARIZONA

Santa Fe

Grand Canyon

Santa Fe is the only railroad entering this National Park

Colorful posters were part of the Santa Fe's promotional machine that marketed the national park, above. Grand Canyon National Park Museum

The Spanish conquistadors, led by Francisco Vásquez de Coronado, were the first Europeans to lead an expedition into what is now the American Southwest. Coronado was searching for the riches of the fabled Seven Cities of Cibola. The quest for bejeweled cities failed, but stories of a great river intrigued Coronado. He dispatched García Lopez de Cárdenas to find the river that cut through what the Spanish considered the disappointingly barren landscape. Cárdenas, with Hopi guides, is credited as the first European to view the Grand Canyon in 1540, somewhere along the South Rim. Cárdenas may have been impressed, but he was not in search of staggering beauty—rather, a route to the Gulf of California. Thwarted by the massive obstacle, he returned to Mexico City with nothing to show for his efforts.

It wasn't until 1776 that the canyon came under a higher calling, when Spanish missionary Francisco Tomás Garcés viewed the Grand Canyon.

Garcés' journals document the people, and his route and reaction to the canyon.

New Spain continued to control the region until the revolution that secured Mexican independence in 1821. The canyon remained the territory of Mexico from 1821 until the end of the Mexican-American War, after which the Territory of New Mexico, which included the Grand Canyon, was created in 1850.

Trappers and traders had explored the region, but serious documentation of the river and the canyon would follow. The most important expeditions, led by Major John Wesley Powell, began in 1869 into the Grand Canyon. Powell recorded his findings as he traveled the Colorado River. His work not only provided the first real information on the uncharted territory, but also introduced its mysteries to the American public. What words could not explain, artists captured.

Landscape artist Thomas Moran's *Chasm of the Colorado,* painted in 1873-1874, and his illustrations for Powell's reports were among the works that struck the public's fancy. Naturalist and conservationist John Muir traveled to the canyon and called it "God's spectacle," while naturalist John Burroughs described it as the "divine abyss."

The old interpretation of the canyon as an obstacle soon transformed into one of opportunity. Copper mining districts opened near the Grand Canyon in the 1870s, but mining was a dangerous and difficult undertaking. There was other profit to be had at the Grand Canyon. Miners and trappers put aside their picks and traps and began catering to the budding tourist trade and became outfitters, guides and innkeepers. Small hotels and cabins, serviced by stage lines, were the first tourist accommodations. Early tourists stayed at the Grandview Hotel, built in 1895 eleven miles east of the South Rim, and Bright Angel Hotel and tent camp built soon after on the South Rim.

On September 17, 1901, the first passenger train chugged from Williams, Arizona,

The Santa Fe and Fred Harvey Co. produced brochures illustrating both the exotic—Hopi House and the Native Americans creating crafts—and the more familiar features like El Tovar hotel, May 1929.

Grand Canyon Museum Collection, No. 17016

The rich tones of the canyon, seen near Yaki Point, define the region's color palette, right. David Morris

to the South Rim of the Grand Canyon. The Santa Fe Railway acquired a bankrupt train line from Williams to Anita Junction, Arizona, and completed the spur to the South Rim. Passengers transferred at Williams from the Santa Fe's intercontinental line onto The Grand Canyon Railway, whose trains departed daily for the three-hour trip to the South Rim.

The train and tourists arrived at a destination ripe for first class development. The railway saw the success of rival Northern Pacific's interests at Yellowstone National Park, and they projected even more visitors to the panoramic vistas of the Grand Canyon—a region that could accommodate tourists year round. The Northern Pacific's Old Faithful Inn opened in June 1904, and the Santa Fe's El Tovar welcomed its first guests seven months later.

As with most of the West, preservation and exploitation ran neck-and-neck. President Benjamin Harrison secured the Grand Canyon Forest Reserve in 1893, but it would be nearly three decades before the

stunning reaches of the Grand Canyon got full national park status.

President Theodore Roosevelt's 1903 visit to the Grand Canyon gave the American people an idea of just what that huge chasm in the seemingly barren high desert of Arizona was all about: "In the Grand Canyon, Arizona has a natural wonder which, so far as I know, is in kind absolutely unparalleled throughout the rest of the world. I want to ask you to do one thing in connection with it in your own interest and in the interest of the country— to keep this great wonder of nature as it is now....I hope you will not have a building of any kind, not a summer cottage, a hotel or anything else, to mar the wonderful grandeur, the sublimity, the great loveliness and beauty of the Canyon. Leave it as it is. You cannot improve on it."

In 1906, Roosevelt created the Grand Canyon Game Reserve by executive order. That same year, he signed the Antiquities Act, which gave him legislative authority to establish Grand Canyon National Monu-

President Teddy Roosevelt, astride a mule in 1913, above, championed for the creation of the Grand Canyon National Monument.
Grand Canyon Museum Collection, No. 1573

Touring cars delivered visitors to El Tovar, where they got a very different experience of the Roaring '20s, facing page. Grand Canyon Museum Collection, No. 9654

A young woman dressed in Victorian "outdoor" attire poses on the rim, 1910, above.
Grand Canyon Museum Collection, No.114

Touring buses brought nattily outfitted guests to El Tovar in 1932, facing page.
Grand Canyon Museum Collection, No. 4653

ment two years later. He also enlarged the forest reserve into a national forest, all before Arizona statehood in 1912. By the time the Grand Canyon became a national park in 1919 under the presidency of Woodrow Wilson, the South Rim had already been developed, and the Santa Fe's El Tovar stood as the flagship hotel of Grand Canyon Village.

Night casts a spell on El Tovar. Amfac Parks and Resorts

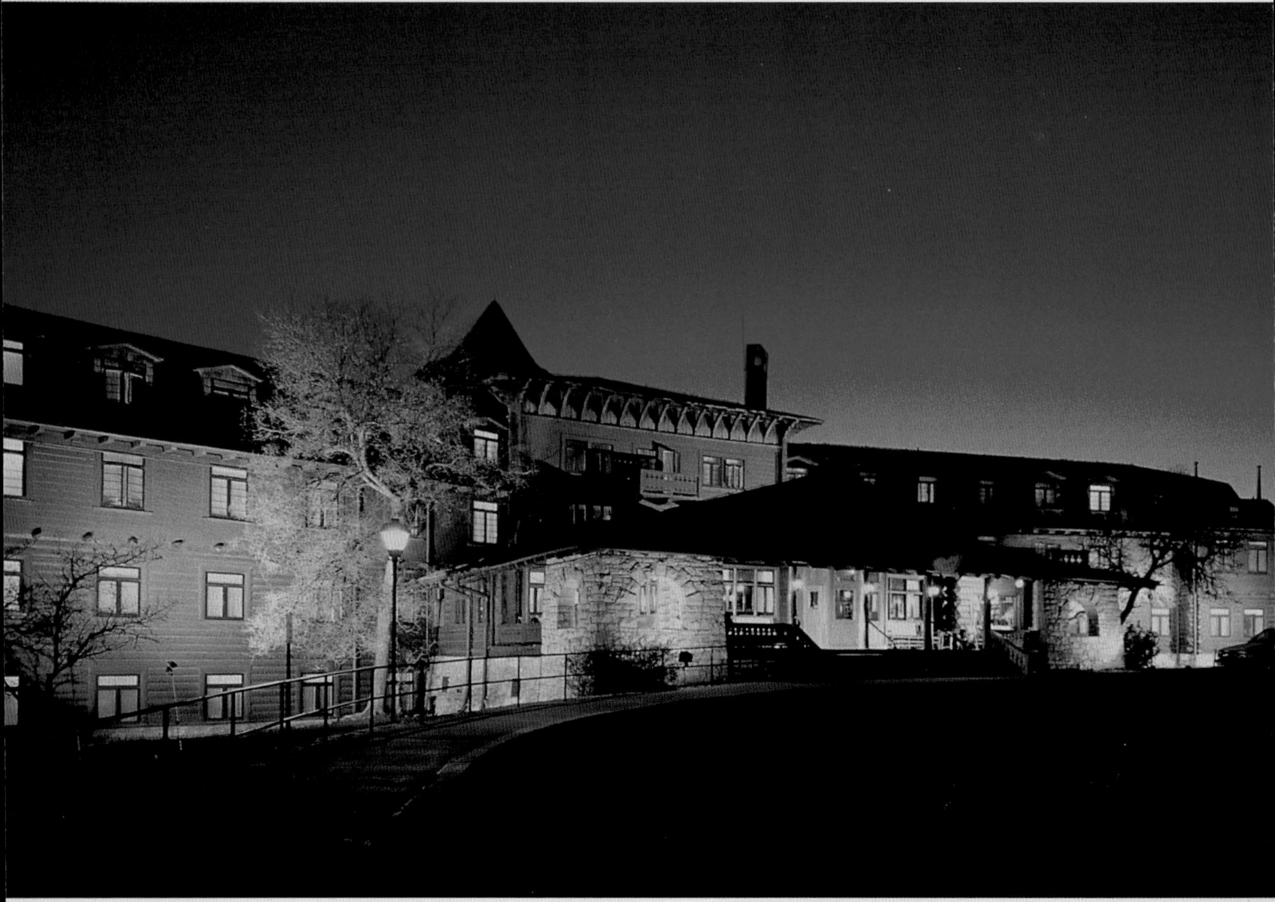

And what a hotel it was! Newspaper accounts stated that "The building itself will be worth a trip to the canyon," and the architecture was described as a combination of "Swiss chateaux" and "castles of the Rhine." Even with its shingle-wrapped turret (water storage tank) and elegant interior solariums and lounges, it evoked the mood of the West that the Santa Fe was promoting.

The combination of cultures was not by chance; architect Charles Whittlesey, who had designed other hotels and stations on the Santa Fe line, saw an opportunity to meld the elegance of a European villa with an American hunting lodge. El Tovar's architecture incorporates the social transition of the era. Part Victorian resort and part rustic log cabin, it provided both the comforts of the known, established eastern resorts and the excitement of the unknown West.

Initial plans called for a more modest hotel, but by May 1902, the *Coconino Sun* reported that Whittlesey had been instructed to double the size of the hotel. Dubbed Bright Angel Tavern during the planning stages, its name was changed before opening to the more suitable El Tovar Hotel, in keeping with the Santa Fe's tradition of naming its hotels of the region after Spanish explorers. The Santa Fe had already named its Trinidad, Colorado, hotel after Cárdenas, so Pedro de Tobar received the honor. Tobar never actually got to the South Rim of the canyon with the Coronado expedition. No matter, the "b" in his name was changed to a "v" (the antique Spanish spelling also eliminated the possible mispronunciation of "to-the-bar" that the Santa Fe feared). Plans for an October completion were delayed, but the grand hotel was officially named and opened on January 14, 1905.

The opening of El Tovar doubled the number of guestrooms available at the South Rim, and its elegance and amenities accentuated the shabbiness of the other hotels. Steam heat, electric lights and indoor plumbing all added up to make it "the most expensively constructed and appointed log house in America." Huge Douglas-firs were shipped by rail from Oregon, pushing the cost of the hotel to $250,000, a grand sum, especially when compared to Old Faithful Inn, built for $140,000. One hundred guestrooms accommodated up to 250 guests who found comfort in "a quiet dignity, an unassuming luxury, and an appreciation of outing needs" at El Tovar.

As described in a promotional brochure of the time, the hotel was "Not a Waldorf-Astoria—admirable as that type is for the city—but a big country clubhouse, where the traveler seeking high-class accommodations also finds freedom from ultra fashionable restrictions. You may wear a dress suit at dinner or not. You may mix with the jolly crowd or sit alone in a quiet nook. Good fellowship perhaps best expresses the motto of El Tovar."

All of this for $3.50 to $4.50 a day on an American plan.

In 1909-10, the railway built the train station (designed by Santa Barbara architect Francis Wilson) just below the hotel, but past any competing businesses. Large copper letters spelling out "Grand Canyon" were placed under the gable of the log depot. Guests arrived at the platform and looked up at the solariums, rooftop

In 1909-10, the railway built the train depot just below El Tovar. Viewed from below, the hotel took on the appearance of a European resort set in the "wild" West, facing page. David Morris

A restored 1959 diesel engine stops at the Grand Canyon Depot, right, while the 185-ton, 1906, Engine 29 pulls Pullman cars from Williams to the South Rim.

Grand Canyon Railway

Today the Rotunda is still "where all paths intersect," facing page. Fred Pflughoft & David Morris

porches with ten-foot posts topped with trefoils, and the turret of El Tovar—the European castle. Then they proceeded up a winding road to the main entrance and ascended the wide steps onto the verandah. Log beams and columns, mission-style stone corner walls with arched openings, and a gable roof, all evoked El Tovar's other personality: the log cabin.

The exterior of the hotel reflects the same juxtaposition of style, heritage and design. The view from the rim shows the log-slab sheathed dining, kitchen and utility wing, extending the cabin image, while gazebos off the

The front desk in the Rotunda has changed little since this bellboy posed there in 1905. Grand Canyon Museum Collection, No. 9453

north porch offer more refined shelter. A much-loved quote from C.A. Higgins' booklet *The Titan of Chasms* appears on the lintel above the porch: "Dreams of mountains, as in their sleep they brood on things eternal."

El Tovar was built on a precipice with one corner just twenty feet from the canyon rim at 7,000-foot elevation. The location of the hotel and access to it by guests was meant as a buildup to the "surprise of the supreme moment," viewing the canyon itself. "It is not until the sightseer reaches the edge that the full force of the view strikes him with a shock

The turret of El Tovar camouflages the water storage tank, above. David Morris

that makes him gasp," exclaimed a 1905 Santa Fe Railway brochure.

The hotel's architecture is notable in the way it blends with the remarkable setting. Stained dark brown, the building, when caught in the late day sun's golden rays, is washed with the same rich hues that bathe the canyon plummeting below. The massive hotel with its varied rooflines seems to sink into the landscape.

Inside, the architect repeated the split personality of the hotel. On the one hand, El Tovar offers old-world charm; on the other hand, there is a heavy dose of rusticity. Stepping through the entrance one enters the main lounge, once called Nimrod's Cabin. Also dubbed the Rendezvous Room, the forty-one-by-thirty-seven-foot space is a hunting lodge personified. Dark-stained log-slab walls, heavy beams and rafters, a stone fireplace in the corner, and polished wood floors are the backdrop for the décor lighted with electric fixtures.

"On the upper shelf repose heads of the deer, elk, moose, mountain sheep, and buffalo, mingling with curiously shaped, and gaudily-tinted Indian jars from the Southwest pueblos," a 1909 brochure described the scene. The furniture was Arts and Crafts design, some later identified as Gustav Stickley. "Nothing cheap

nor tawdry is tolerated," boasted the brochure.

In the center of the building is the registration lobby, or Rotunda, where "all paths intersect." The log-fronted registration desk has changed little, and the Mezzanine Lounge above it has an octagonal balcony with Swiss-styled jigsawn balustrades. This was the crimson-draped Ladies Lounge where "...the better half of

The arched rockwork, top photo David Morris, *lends elegance to the log exterior of the hotel also seen in the 1904 photograph taken soon after El Tovar was completed, above.* Grand Canyon Museum Collection, No. 9835
The exterior deck detailing illustrates the Swiss influence of the hotel's design, facing page. Fred Pflughoft

the world may see without being seen—may chat and gossip—may sew and read—may do any of the inconsequent nothings which serve to pleasantly pass the time away."

Music and dancing were enjoyed in the ivory and gold trimmed Music Room with a view of the canyon; billiards, pool and cards were played in the ground-level Amusement Room; libation was taken by gentlemen in the Grotto; ladies "sun bathed" in the wicker filled Sun Parlor; and elegant meals, prepared by an "Italian chef, once employed in New York and Chicago clubs," were served in the eighty-nine-foot-long dining room, where the famed "Harvey Girls" waited tables.

A richly paneled, private dining room was (and still is) available for intimate dinners. The story goes that the room was specifically added for Teddy Roosevelt, who liked to show up for dinner in his muddy boots and riding gear.

The kitchen of El Tovar has always prepared notable cuisine. A herd of Jersey cows and a poultry farm supplied fresh milk, butter and eggs. The hotel had its own bakery, butcher shop and bulk storage refrigerators to keep Pacific salmon, California fruit, Kansas beef and imported cheeses. Dignitaries and celebrities were often guests, and the staff went whole hog with their preparations. The 1909 dinner honoring President Taft and party, given by Governor Sloan of Arizona, featured: Fresh Caviar; Consomme Alice; Crab Flakes, Salamander; Breast of Mountain Grouse, Truffled; Heart of Artichoke; Roast Saddle of Venison; Sweet Potatoes; El Tovar Salad; Nesselrode Pudding, Sauce Sabayon; assorted Cakes; Roquefort and Sierra Cheeses and Coffee.

The Santa Fe Railway alone was not responsible for the success of El Tovar. The Fred Harvey Company managed the hotel, along with other railway properties. Fred Harvey had opened his first restaurant at the Santa Fe Depot in Topeka, Kansas, in 1876, before the addition of dining cars to trains. What followed was a thriving business with restaurants built by the

The original Arts and Crafts dining room décor was replaced by more elegant furniture, and four murals depicting Indian tribes of the region were added to the massive room. Fred Pflughoft & David Morris

railway along the Santa Fe lines through Colorado, Kansas, Texas, New Mexico, Arizona, California and Alabama, and managed by Fred Harvey.

Food and service were foremost, and the famed Harvey Girl waitresses began working in 1883. The hard working, well-trained and strictly chaperoned young women drew quite a following. (In the 1940s, Metro-Goldwyn-Mayer released a musical, *The Harvey Girls*, starring Judy Garland, Angela Lansbury and Preston Wills.)

The senior Harvey died in 1901 before El Tovar opened, but his sons continued managing the South Rim facilities, purchasing them from the Santa Fe in 1954. The Fred Harvey Company became a subsidiary of Amfac, Inc., in 1968.

The Santa Fe Railway and Fred Harvey Company together blazed a new trail in advertising and marketing of merchandise in conjunction with their train lines, stations and destination facilities. They introduced images of the Southwest and

Indian arts, jewelry, rugs and basketry to the
rest of the country at world fairs and expositions, as well as in retail concerns. The
Santa Fe hired and promoted artists and
photographers, including Thomas Moran,
to capture the beauty of the Southwest.

Expositions were the rage, and the Santa
Fe and Fred Harvey Company took full
advantage of the venues to bring the
Southwest to the masses. Their efforts for
the 1915 San Francisco Panama-Pacific
International Exposition were grandiose if
not as grand as the canyon itself. "The
Grand Canyon of Arizona" six-acre exhibit
included an Indian village plus a replica of
the canyon to be viewed from cars that
carried tourists along the "rim" for 25
cents a trip.

Under the direction of the railway's
general advertising agent, William
Simpson, the company acquired a vast art
collection and became a corporate patron
of the arts. Included was the 1907 Louis
Akin painting "El Tovar Hotel, Grand
Canyon." As early as 1902, the Indian

Department of the Fred Harvey Company
began collecting Native American art and
artifacts to sell in its shops and to use for
decorating.

The Santa Fe and Harvey Company
strove to monopolize the South Rim's
"entertainment." Guests wanted more
than to view the canyon from the rim, but
others had already built trails and operated
guided trips. The Santa Fe's solution was
to acquire access then construct a trail and
road of its own. "Trail Drives and Saddle
Horses" were advertised in their 1912
brochures. The hotel provided divided
skirts for the women and leggings for the
men if they were not prepared for the ride.

The railway brought more than tourists
and supplies to the park. During its
heyday, when El Tovar needed to be
reshingled, the railroad brought in a train
of work and tool cars that housed the
"B&B Gang," or Bridges and Buildings.
When El Tovar needed repainting, a
different train came in that housed the
Paint Gang, and so on.

In 1989, after twenty-one years without train service, the renovated Grand Canyon Railway brought tourists back to the South Rim "the old fashioned way"— by steam engine, left. *Al Richmond*
In so doing, owners of the railway, Max and Thelma Biegert, resurrected a chunk of Arizona history. Trains leave the restored Williams Depot, right, and after 65 miles of pine forests, high desert plains and endless vistas, they arrive at Grand Canyon Depot. The rail line is on the National Register of Historic Places.
Grand Canyon Railway

Custom-made furniture in the Rendezvous Room was part of extensive redecorating that brought back the original essence of the lobby.
Fred Pflughoft & David Morris

While early travelers embraced rail travel, by 1926 more visitors were arriving by private car than Pullman car. The historic depot closed in 1968, and El Tovar was showing serious signs of aging.

Major rehabilitation projects costing millions of dollars have brought the grande dame of the South Rim back to life and kept it well preserved.

In 1975, the first stage of a two-part renovation was celebrated when a new heating/cooling system and kitchen were installed and the principal suites redecorated. Then-governor of Arizona Raul Castro cited the importance of El Tovar to the state's tourism industry and said, "As El Tovar goes, so goes Arizona's tourist trade."

Additional interior remodeling and a $1.5 million rehabilitation of the exterior, which included insulation and replacement of windows with thermal panes and brown-tone aluminum frames, began in 1981. Fifty to sixty percent of the rotting exterior logs and wooden decking on

El Tovar's exterior reflects the juxtaposition of style, heritage and design. The log-slab dining wing with stone chimney creates the cabin image, while gazebos and turrets offer a more refined look. Fred Pflughoft

balconies and porches was replaced. The renovation was completed in 1983.

Remodeling of the main dining room made it more elegant than the original design. The huge room (three times the size of the Rendezvous Room) has two stone chimneys, one on the north and one on the south, each flanked by large picture windows. Four large murals by Brue Himeche depict the customs of four Indian tribes: the Hopi, Apache, Mojave, and Navajo. The simple Arts and Crafts period chairs and tables were replaced with elegant armchairs. Stained-glass lights now hang instead of the original log chandeliers. A side porch was converted to the Canyon Dining Room, where a 1920 Chris Jorgenson painting hangs opposite the bank of windows facing the rim. Porches along the dining room were later additions.

There are now seventy-eight guestrooms, each with a private bath. What was the Amusement Room still has the rubble masonry walls with elegant arched openings that replicate the arches at the front of the building, but the pool and card tables have been replaced by public restrooms, phone banks and storage facilities. And today, even those who don't qualify as "ladies" can enjoy the Mezzanine Lounge.

Another million-dollar renovation of El Tovar took place while the hotel was closed for two months in the winter of 1998. Sixty-six guestrooms were refurnished with reproductions of period décor, the rooms and hallways carpeted and bathrooms tiled in heritage hexagon tiles. Twelve suites, named after Grand Canyon legends like Charles Whittlesey, Fred Harvey and Mary Jane Colter, have also been refurbished. The kitchen was remodeled and, along with its new look, the restaurant updated its menu.

After all of this work, El Tovar maintains the aristocratic atmosphere and Western intrigue it was intended to evoke as a destination for the elite.

Architect Mary Jane Colter's work, under the direction of the Fred Harvey Company, included the Hopi House built across from El Tovar, below. *Fred Pflughoft*

Colter also designed cabins as part of Bright Angel Camp on the South Rim, facing page, *Amfac Parks and Resorts*

Other Historic Structures

The park's early architecture reflected the style of native peoples along with rustic "parkitecture" developed by the National Park Service. Hopi House, designed by Mary Jane Colter, a onetime Minnesota drawing and design teacher, opened just prior to El Tovar. Built to replicate a Hopi pueblo, its multiple roofs and sandstone walls with tiny windows offered the perfect venue for the Harvey museum collection of Navajo blankets. Indian artisans produced jewelry, pottery, blankets and other artwork and trinkets for sale. Tourists could watch the Indians at work, and were entertained in the evening with Hopi singing and traditional dancing.

Hopi House was the first of a series of work Colter produced as architect and interior designer for Fred Harvey Company. El Tovar was the compound's flagship, but Colter's design and decorating work fills the area. In 1914, Colter designed Hermit's Rest along the Santa Fe's trail into the canyon. The one-time rest stop is tucked into a man-made mound and from the outside seems like a rustic protrusion. Inside, a large porch, huge fireplace within a stone arch, and oversized glass windows refine the structure. That same year, The Lookout Studio was built west of El Tovar as a viewpoint of the canyon and shop to sell postcards, photo-

Phantom Ranch, above, built at the end of the eight-mile Kaibab Trail at the bottom of the canyon opened in 1922. Its architect, Mary Jane Colter, and her sister road mules to what has become a favorite destination for hikers and rafters. Amfac Parks and Resorts
Colter also designed Bright Angel Lodge, facing page. David Morris

graphs and art work. Other Colter buildings at the Grand Canyon include: Phantom Ranch eight miles into the canyon, 1922; Watchtower, at the end of East Rim Drive, 1932; Bright Angel Lodge, designed as an economy lodge with surrounding cabins to replace the original Bright Angel

Camp, 1935; Men's Dormitory, 1936; and Women's Dormitory, 1937.

On the North Rim of the Grand Canyon, today a five-hour drive from the South Rim, the Union Pacific Railroad hired architect Gilbert Stanley Underwood to design Grand Canyon Lodge as part of its

On the North Rim, a five-hour drive from El Tovar, the Union Pacific Railroad built Grand Canyon Lodge. Grand Canyon Museum Collection, No. 8127

The Watchtower, Mary Jane Colter's 1932 masterpiece, was patterned after ancient towers and kivas and decorated with Indian cave and wall drawings, facing page. Amfac Parks and Resorts

such individual designations in the park including El Tovar, Lookout Studio, Hopi House, Hermit's Rest and Watchtower along with the Grand Canyon Depot and Grand Canyon Lodge. Many others are on the National Register of Historic Buildings.

With the establishment of the region as a national park, the newly formed National Park Service (1916)

"Loop Tour" connecting it to the railroad's Utah facilities. The 1928 masterpiece burned in 1932, but was rebuilt on the original stone foundation and stands in the less accessible north side of the park.

Grand Canyon Village, on the South Rim, received its designation as a National Historic Landmark in 1997. There are ten

constructed housing and administrative buildings, most in the rustic "parkitecture" style. Roads were gradually paved, private interests eliminated, and park boundaries adjusted. During the Great Depression, Civilian Conservation Corps built trails and campgrounds.

On the South Rim, Sinking Ship seems to slip under a wave of sky. David Morris

Clouds gather over the North Rim from Cape Royal, below.
The sun peeks over the horizon at Hopi Point, facing page. David Morris

Grand Canyon National Park

In 1919, the first year that Grand Canyon was a national park, 44,173 visitors came to see the latest addition to America's national park system. By 1956, visitorship passed the one million mark, and in 1969 over two million tourists came to the park. In 1998, nearly five million people visited the park, and most traveled to the South Rim.

Early problems of roaming cattle, sewage disposal and lack of zoning were periodically replaced with new challenges that came with the growth and development of Grand Canyon Village. By 1924, the NPS and Santa Fe Railway devised a master plan for development of the South Rim, the most traveled portion of the park. Since then it has been a work in progress.

The South Rim is only a small dot on the 1,218,376 acres of Grand Canyon National Park. Besides the huge influx of tourists and staff, 88 species of mammals, 287 different birds, 25 kinds of fishes and 50 species of reptiles and amphibians call the park home. Vegetation ranges from Ponderosa and piñon pine forest of the plateau region to cacti and other desert plants of the canyon floor. The canyon floor follows the cut of the Colorado River for 277 miles beginning at Lees Ferry and ending at Grand Wash Cliffs. The entire park is a World Heritage Site.

In 1989 the Grand Canyon Railway line again began moving passengers from Williams to the South Rim. The train

Mules are still a favored form of transportation into the canyon, above. Amfac Parks and Resorts
Vishnu Temple as seen from Cape Royal, facing page. David Morris

departs daily from the historic 1908 Williams Depot for a two hour and fifteen minute ride in refurbished Harriman-style Pullman cars pulled by historic steam locomotives in the summer, with 1950-vintage diesel engines for winter runs. The line is along the original rail bed, all painstakingly rebuilt.

Tourists at the turn-of-the-20th-century wanted to explore the inner canyon, as do travelers of the 21st century. A trip to the bottom of the canyon and back (on foot or by mule) takes two days. Rim-to-rim hikers generally spend three days one-way to get from the North Rim to the South Rim. A trip through Grand Canyon by raft can take two weeks or longer.

In 1995 the Grand Canyon National Park General Management Plan was approved. It was the culmination of a four-year process that involved local citizens, American Indian tribes, and public and private agencies.

The plan is just that—a plan—to guide the management of resources, visitor use,

The park's landscape includes piñon pine and lichen-covered rock, *above.* David Morris
The subdued remnants of the evening's sunset caught looking east from Hopi Point, *previous page.* David Morris

and general development at the park over a ten- to fifteen-year period with the goal of protecting park resources while providing for meaningful visitor experiences. A secondary purpose is to encourage compatible activities on adjacent lands so as to minimize negative effects on the park.

As stated by the National Park Service: "Implementing a general management plan for a park like Grand Canyon is not a static process. The park service must adapt to the realities brought about by implementation and 'adjust' the GMP accordingly. The final plan is programmatic and conceptual, with site-specific

The strength of El Tovar's design is the blending of architecture and landscape. David Morris

planning and compliance conducted as need for implementation."

Grand Canyon National Park is a designated natural wonder. Our national parks hold both natural and cultural beauty. Man can never match the majesty of such a place, but El Tovar, the lumbering creation of architect Charles Whittlesey, conceived and built by a great railway, managed by an innovative family company, and enjoyed by guests from presidents to movie stars, is a wonder in itself.

Sunset washes the canyon's North Rim, left, while Vishnu Temple is silhouetted in the first light of day, above. David Morris

Selected Bibliography

The author wishes to thank the architects, historians and archivists with the National Park Service, particularly Kim Besom, Gordon Chappell, Sara Stebbins and Joanne Wilkins, and Bob Baker of Grand Canyon National Park Lodges.

Day breaks gently off Hopi Point. David Morris

Albright, Horace and Robert Cahn. *The Birth of the National Park Service: The Founding Years, 1913-33* (Salt Lake City, 1985).

Anderson, Michael. *Living at the Edge* (Grand Canyon, 1998).

Barnes, Christine. *Great Lodges of the West* (Bend, Oregon, 1997).

Bradley, Glen. *The Story of the Santa Fe* (Boston, 1930, reprinted, 1995).

D'Emillo, Sandra and Suzan Campbell. *Visions & Visionaries: The Art and Artists of the Santa Fe Railway* (Salt Lake City, 1991).

Grattan, Virginia L. *Mary Colter: Builder Upon the Red Earth* (Flagstaff, 1980).

Hughes, Donald, J. *In the House of Stone and Light* (Grand Canyon, 1991).

Kaiser, Harvey H. *Landmarks in the Landscape* (San Francisco, 1997).

Kampes, Leslie Polling. *The Harvey Girls* (New York, 1989).

Richmond, Al. *The Story of the Grand Canyon Railway* (Grand Canyon Railway, revised 1995).

Reports: Harrison, Laura Soulliere, National Register of Historic Places Inventory Nomination Form, El Tovar and Indian

Watchtower at Desert View, Lookout Studio, Hopi House, Hermit's Rest (National Park Service, Southwest Regional Office, 1986). Tweed, William; Laura E. Soulliere; Henry G. Law. National Park Service Rustic Architecture: 1916-1942, (National Park Service, Western Regional Office, Feb. 1977).

Grand Canyon National Park Museum Collection, Grand Canyon, AZ. History file: *El Tovar: A New Hotel at the Grand Canyon of Arizona*, 1909; *Hotel El Tovar*, 1905; *Titan of the Chasms: The Grand Canyon of Arizona*, 1904; *Doing the Grand Canyon*, 1909; Correspondence: Atchison, Topeka & Santa Fe, 1902-11; *Arizona Daily Sun*, April 1, 1975, Sept. 8, 1975, Nov. 1, 1981; Superintendent's Annual Reports, 1919-1920, 1920-21, 1926-28, 1932, 1936; Grand Canyon Lodge, North Rim file: *The Hotel in the Wilderness*, author unknown; UP Railroad promotional brochures, 1928-32. History file, Fred Harvey Company: The Fred Harvey Collection: 1889-1963; AmFac, Inc. press release, July 10, 1968. Historic photo collection.

Hotel Reservations

El Tovar and all in-park lodging is available through Grand Canyon National Park Lodges; call (520) 638-2631 for same-day reservations or (303) 297-2757 for advance reservations. El Tovar is open year round. www.amfac.com

Directions

El Tovar is located in Grand Canyon Village (South Rim), 60 miles north of Interstate 40 at Williams via highway 64, and 80 miles northwest of Flagstaff via highway 180.

The Grand Canyon Railway runs daily departing from Williams, Arizona, to the South Rim of the Grand Canyon. For information on tours call 1-800-843-8724.

Grand Canyon National Park Website: www.nps.gov.grca

A Technicolor sunset display off Bright Angel Point, following page. David Morris